GOD IS REAL

DEMETERIUS MEYERS

KENTISH PUBLISHING COMPANY ©

GOD IS REAL
Copyright © 2019 Demeterius Meyers

Published in Raleigh, North Carolina, by Kentish Publishing Company. Kentish Publishing is a registered trademark of Kentish Publishing Company.

Kentish Publishing Company titles may be purchased in bulk for ministry, educational, business, fund-raising, or sales promotional use.

www.kentishpublishing.com

Scripture taken from the New King James Version®. Copyright © 1982 by Thomas Nelson. Used by permission. All rights reserved.

Scripture quotations marked (NLT) are taken from the Holy Bible, New Living Translation, copyright © 1996, 2004, 2007, 2013, 2015 by Tyndale House Foundation. Used by permission of Tyndale House Publishers, Inc., Carol Stream, Illinois 60188. All rights reserved.

THE HOLY BIBLE, NEW INTERNATIONAL VERSION®, NIV® Copyright © 1973, 1978, 1984, 2011 by Biblica, Inc.® Used by permission. All rights reserved worldwide.

Graphics © 2019 Esther Ruth Kentish

ISBN 978-1-7339115-0-4

Printed in the United States of America

DEDICATION

I would like to dedicate this book to God, because without Him I am nothing.

ACKNOWLEDGMENTS

First, I would like to thank God because without Him I am nothing, but with Him and through Him I am everything. To my family and friends (mom, dad, sister, brother, and cousins) thank you, for your encouragement and support. Your love and support mean more to me than you will ever know. To my daughter, Nyarie Asante' Warren thank-you for being patient; while, God showed me how to be a Godly mother. I love you more than words can express. Last but certainly not least, to my fiancé. I want to thank you for your support. You never doubted me and when I would reach a bump in the road you would say, "It's a small thing to a giant." I have a great support team. We are faith walkers.

Thank you!

TABLE OF CONTENTS

1   Who am I? God of Creation

2   Who am I? God of Love

3   Who am I? God of Peace

4   Who am I? God of Power

5   Who am I? God of Praise

6   Who am I? God of Vision

7   Who am I? God of Completion

8   Who am I? God of Faith

9   Who am I? God of Prayer

10   Who am I? God of Provision

PROLOGUE

Hi, I am Ruth Brown, my husband is Kevin Brown, and Elise Brown is our daughter. It all began when we took Elise to children's church. Everyday thereafter, her mind never stopped wanting to learn more about Christ. See, as parents, I know we were raised by our parents teaching us to do as I say and not as I do.

Well, with these millennium babies this does not work. They watch every move you make and will ask you about it. They are fearless and faithful to what they love. As you will quickly learn, they are definitely on another level. Elise is a very inquisitive six-year-old that lives with her mother and father. Through their conversations, you will learn that God is *Real,* and He will give you the words to say.

I was only a baby in Christ and there were so many times I did not know what to say when Elise asked me about God. **BUT** God always downloaded into my spirit what to say and what not to say. This little girl made me stay on my knees and it wasn't until then I learned that God was the *Real* Deal!

7

Chapter 1

Who am I?

God of Creation

"In the beginning God created the heavens and the earth."

Genesis: 1: 1

Mom walks in the room. Elise is sitting there in the corner crying. Mom kneels down near her and whispers,

"Beautiful, what's wrong?"

Elise looks up at her mom with her pretty brown eyes filled with tears and says,

"I just don't get it! I just don't get it!"

Mom says, "Get what, get what Elise?"

She says, "God."

Mom pauses and says, "Well, let me help you. God is omnipotent."

Elise says, "Huh? Mom, I'm only six, what does that big word mean?"

Mom says, "Sorry, girly. It means that He is everywhere all at once."

Elise, says "Ooooh, like Santa Clause."

Mom giggles slightly and responds,

"Ummm, not quite. He knows all and sees all, but He is a supernatural being." Mom looks at Elise to read her facial expression and says, "Do you remember the Creation story you learned in Sunday school?

Elise jumps up and says, "YES, YES, I do! It says, in the beginning God created the heavens and earth.

Mom says, "Correct..."

Elise interrupts and says, "Ms. Edwards taught us that He created the whole world in seven days and then rested."

"That is correct," Mom says with a pleasant smile on her face.

Elise, "And, and, and, He rests on the seventh day."

Mom says, "That is correct. So, baby girl, the first thing that you need to know about God is that He created this whole world and He is everywhere."

Elise says, "Okay…" she pauses and says, "Welllllllll, I still have more questions, but they can wait."

Mom says, "That will be fine. We can talk about who people say and believe that He is.

Elise says, "Sure, sure I was just crying because I love Him so much and even though I am six years old I want to understand who He is."

Mom says, "Well, you remember what I told you. You should pray always, and He will help you even if you do not know what to say. Just PRAY!"

Mom also tells her that as you get older you will understand who He is to you but know for now that He is the creator of all things. Elise, nods and says,

"Yes, ma'am, Creator of all things. That's who He is," and she hugs her mom tightly.

Prayer: Dear God, help me to know you. Amen

Chapter 2
Who am I?

God of Love

"For God so loved the world that He gave his only begotten Son that whosoever believes in him should not perish and will everlasting life." John 3:16

Elise and her mom are riding down the street on their way home. Elise is sitting in the back seat looking out of the window and Mom is driving listening to their favorite gospel artist *Mary, Mary*. Mom is singing, and Elise is in the back trying to keep up with her mom singing. As they ride, Elise says,

"Mom, what do you mean when you say God is love? I hear you say it all the time, and I heard you and Daddy talking."

Mom, smiles as she normally does when Elise asks a question and says,

"When I say God is love, I mean that everything that you do, you should do it out of love. Do you remember the first scripture I taught you?"

Elise says, "Umm yes, I think so."

Mom says, "Okay, say what you remember."

Elise says, "Oookay, For God so loved the world…" Elise stops.

Mom says, "Okay, finish it."

Elise says, "Ummmm, ummmm…" and shrugs her shoulders slowly and says, "I can't remember." She grabs her cheeks and yells, "Oh no, oh no, I can't remember!"

Mom says, "Calm down. Let me help you. It says, 'For God so loved the world that He gave his only begotten Son that whosoever believes in Him should not perish but have everlasting life.'" Mom pauses and let out a sigh, and says, "Now that's love."

Elise says, "Yes, now I remember, "'For God so loved the world that he gave his only begotten son that whooooosoever believes in Him should not perish but have everlasting life.'" Elise yells, "So God gave his son away! Wow, Mama, that *is* love. If a man can do this for us and not know us…"

Elise sits quietly in the back. Mom sits quietly as well, because they are in their driveway. They both sit very still.

Mom interrupts the silence and says, "Okay, Pumpkin, let's get out, but remember this: no matter what you do in life, if you are doing it out of love, then you won't go wrong because God is love!"

Elise, nods as usual and says, "Mom, I love you."

Mom says, "I love you too, baby girl. Now, let's go inside."

Elise says, "Okay, but you know I still have more questions." Mom giggles and nods at the same time

"…Oh, of course. Don't I know."

Prayer: Dear God, thank you for showing us what love is, and teach me how to love like you. Amen.

Chapter 3

Who am I?
God of Peace

"And the peace of God which surpasses all understanding will guard your hearts and minds through Christ Jesus." Philippians 4:7

It's Saturday morning and Elise and her Mom are in the kitchen. Mom has just finished cooking breakfast. Elise is having pancakes, bacon, eggs, grits, and orange juice. Meanwhile, Mom is having coffee and Dad is having grape juice. Dad is on his way out and excuses himself from the table.

See, they own a family gas station and it is the end of the month, which means he has to go do inventory. He walks over to the stove where mom is drinking her coffee and just stares at her, grins, and waits until she places her coffee cup on the counter.

He says, "Love you, babe," kissing her on her forehead. He then walks to Elise. He hugs her around her neck and kisses her cheek, "Daddy loves you," he whispers. He then walks out the door.

Mom is cleaning up the kitchen and Elise is still sitting at the table eating and swinging her legs from the chair humming.

Mom says, "Elise, what are you humming, dear?"

Elise says, "Mom, I don't know the name of
the 'church song."

Mom corrects her and says, "You mean *gospel*
song."

Elise says, "Yes, I just keep hearing it. 'He will give
you peace, He will give you peace.' She says,
"Mom, what does it mean when the song says, 'He
is a God of Peace?'

Mom looks at her with a great big smile on her
face, and says, "Do you remember that time you
said the little girl was teasing you in your class?"

Elise looks up at her mom with a sad face and nods
slowly.

She drops her eyes back down quickly.

Mom says, "No sweetie, I wanted to use that as an
example."

Elise holds her head high and says, "Okay."

Mom says, "Remember when I met with your
teacher? Even though Sally was teasing you and
calling you 'church girl', your teacher said you had

a calmness over you even when all of the kids were laughing."

Elise interrupts and says, "Yes, I know she was being mean to me, but I still did not want to be mean to her."

Mama says, "Yes, that is correct."

Elise says, "I just kept hearing you say, 'What would Jesus do?' and that, 'God is Love.' And . . . and, Mama, I knew if I punched her like I wanted to, God wouldn't be pleased with me.

Mama looks away to keep from showing her snicker of a laugh.

She says, "That is correct, and you know what that is called, Elise?"

Elise says, "What, Mama?"

Mama says, "Peace, baby girl."

Elise looks puzzled mumbling, "Ummm . . . peace?"

Mama says, "Let me explain. See, even though you were upset because Sally was picking on you, you said you still could not hit her. The reason why you felt like that is because God gave you that peace. Only God can do that in a situation where people will think you should react a certain way and you don't. *That* is peace. God is a God of peace. He will calm us even when we think we can't be calm."

Elise smiles and says, "Yes, Mama, I get it. I'm glad God gave me a feeling of peace because you know what I wanted to do was . . ."

Mama places one finger over her lips to quiet her and says, "Don't say it, baby girl. Let's just thank God for being a God of peace."

Elise says, "Okay . . . peace."

She gets up from the table, places her dishes in the sink, and asks if she can go in the backyard to jump on her trampoline. Mama says yes.

As Elise is walking out the door, she hums, "He will give you peace, He will give you peace."

Mama looks at her as she closes the door and looks up to the sky and says a thank you to the Lord, The Giver of Peace.

She quickly jumps because she is startled by Elise, who peeks her head back in the doorway and says,

"Mama, you know I have more questions."

Mama says, "Of course you do, dear."

The door slams and mama continues to clean the

kitchen.

Prayer: Thank you God for being the giver of peace.

Amen

Chapter 4

Who am I?
God of Power

"Now unto him that is able to do immeasurably more than all we ask or imagine according to His power that is a work within us." Ephesians 3:20

It is a normal Thursday spring evening; Mom and Elise are on their way to Elise's ballet practice. In the car mom is listening to the song, *There is something about the name of Jesus.* Mom is humming this song and adding her own tunes, saying its power in His name.

Elise is sitting in the back seat looking out the window. As they pass by the stores, other cars, and houses, they pull up in the parking lot. Mom parks the car, sits and rocks, humming until the song stops.

Mom whispers, "Thank you, Jesus."

Elise says, "Thank you, Jesus!"

Mom turns around, looks in the back seat, and smiles at her. "Come on baby, let's go before you are late for practice."

Elise says, "Wait, Mom, I want to ask you something!"

Mom looks at her with a glow in her eye, and a smile on her face.

"Elise," she proceeds to say, "What is God's power? What does that mean?"

Mom says, "Aahhh," and nods as usual. "We, as Christians, experience God's power just because of who He is. I will explain more on our way back home."

Elise says, "Okay, Mama. I asked because I heard you in your bathroom getting dressed and praying to the Lord, 'I thank you for your power in your name,' and I was just wondering.

Mom tilts her head over and grins

"So, you heard me praying?"

Elise nods, "Yes, ma'am, I hear you praying all the time. You always call His name. I hear you say, 'Jesus, Jesus, Jesus.'"

Mom smiles and says, "Yes, you are correct. Come on, you are going to be late. Grab your bag."

"Okay!" Elise's says, and they both walk to the door and, as they walk up the steps, they are greeted by her teacher and some other parents sitting in the lobby.

Mom speaks to the other parents and goes back out to her car to wait for practice to end. While sitting in the car, Mom turns her music back on low and begins to pray.

"Dear God, it's me, your daughter, and I am so thankful for the many blessings you have given me. I am even more thankful for this little girl that you gave me who is really stretching our families' faith. She is so wise, and all I see is you, God. I chose the name Elise. . . Well, you chose the name, but I see why. This name comes from '. . .Elisheba and, in Hebrew, means oath of God, or God is satisfaction.' I know you are truly satisfied, and I truly understand when you say, 'I know the plans I have for you.' You and I both know that I was not planning to have any more children. However, you saw fit to bless us to be a blessing for others, and I can't thank you enough. Now, I'm coming to you asking for more strength to be able to explain your word, and who you are with clarity. It is important that Elise knows you, and who you are for herself, even at a young age. Help me explain your power to her. In Jesus' name, Father, I pray with expectation of clarity from you. Your daughter, Ruth. Amen."

Time has flown by, and mom realizes that it is time to go back inside and get Elise from practice. She walks in and gets her, and they get in the car and drive off.

Mom says, "How was practice?"

Elise says, "It was fun we are learning some new positions. We have a performance coming up and I have the paper in my bag!"

Mom says, "Okay, I will look at it when I get home."

Elise says, "Mom, can you explain what God's power is?"

Mom says, "Yes, baby. God's power is hard to explain, but I will try. It is simple to me now, but as my relationship grew with Him, I realized that it goes back to the first scripture I taught you. God is God all by Himself."

Elise nods silently as her mother continues.

"He is the beginning and the end and because of who He is, there is power in His name. Do you remember your problem at school, and how you received peace because of your situation?"

Elise says, "Yes, well, because of his Supernatural powers, like Batman."

Mom says, "No, no, that is pretend, but our God is Real. He sent His son to die for us, and just because of that we have power when we say His name. When you don't know what to say, just call on His name. Mom begins to say, "Jesus, Jesus, Jesus, Jesus ooooh there is power in His name."

Mom beings to rock slightly as she is driving down the street. Elise is very quiet and does not ask any more questions. She is trying to understand what her mom just told her. As they are riding, and Mama is turning in the neighborhood, Elise is very still and there is a sense of calmness and peace in the car. Mom does not say anything else about the power of God. God's peace is over Elise while in the car.

Mom smiles because she feels His presence and thanks Him for his blessing of understanding. They pull into the driveway and mom says,

"Come on Elise, grab your things, we have to go inside and eat dinner."

Mom and Elise get out of the car and walk inside. Elise hugs her mother tightly and runs in the den where her daddy is watching the game. She is incredibly excited and hugs him tightly as well.

Dad says, "What is that for, baby?"

She says, "No reason. I love you, Daddy."

Her dad smiles as she walks to go wash her hands. He takes a moment and looks to heaven and whispers, "Jesus, Jesus, Jesus."

Prayer: Dear God, thank you for helping me understand the power in your name. Amen

Chapter 5

Who am I?
God of Praise

"Praise ye the Lord, O give thanks unto the Lord for he is good: for his mercy endureth forever." Psalms 106:1

It is Saturday morning choir rehearsal and Elise is sitting in the audience waiting on her mom. The choir is rehearsing in the choir loft, and the director raises his hand to start the performance. The choir stands up and sings, *'Praise is what I do.'*

The choir begins to lift their hands up in the atmosphere in motion with the song, the sound radiates with volume through the empty church. The choir has Elise's full attention. She is staring and humming the lyrics.

The spirit of the Lord is present.

The song has ended, and they close with instructions for Sunday morning and a prayer. Mom walks down from the choir loft, grabs Elise's hand, and tells her,

"We have to pick up some things up for dinner tonight so let's hurry."

Elise says, "Yes, ma'am," and they walk to the car.

Mom and Elise skip to the car singing, *'I'll praise you in the good and in the bad. . .'*

Elise says, "Mom, I like that song."

Mom says, "What song, baby?"

She says, "The one that says, *'Praise is what I do when I don't know what to do.'*"

Mom says, "Oh yeah, that is one of my favorite songs. Let me tell you a story as we ride to the store."

Elise nods and says, "Okay."

They get into the car, buckle up, and mom begins by saying, "When you want to confuse the devil, then you put a praise on it."

Elise giggles and asks, "Put a praise on it? How do you do that?"

Mama smiles and says, "Sorry, I'm using words you are not familiar with, and you are getting confused. See, it is when you feel like things are going bad, and even when they are not going good, you sing praises to God. He likes that, but when you feel like the devil is bothering you, you confuse him by singing praises into his presence. *Psalms 100:4* tells us, *'Enter his gates with thanksgiving and his courts with praise; give thanks to him and praise his name.'* This is a reminder that we should sing to God when we are singing at home, at church, or wherever."

Elise sits quietly and nods as her mother continues, "One good song you can sing is, *'Praise is what I do.'* See, the scripture reminds us to, *'Praise ye the Lord, O give thanks unto the Lord for he is good: for his mercy endureth forever.'* (Psalms 106:1) That means, no matter what, we should sing praises to God."

Elise says, "Oh, I understand Mama, like you and Daddy do in the morning when you are getting ready for work, and at night when you are getting ready for bed."

Mama says, "Yes, that is correct Elise. That would be a form of singing praises to God."

Elise sits back in the car quietly, Mom turns the music back up. Within a few minutes they are at the grocery store.

Mom says, "Okay, Elise, we are here."

Elise says, "Okay," and unbuckles her seatbelt to get out of

the car. She closes the car door and grabs her mom's hand.

Mom locks the car door and looks up to Heaven and smiles.

"Lord, you did it again. Thank you for the gift of praise."

Prayer: Dear God, thank you for the gift of praise. Amen

Chapter 6

Who am I?
God of Vision

*"For I know the plans I have for you," declares the LORD,
"plans to prosper you and not to harm you, plans to give you
hope and a future." Jeremiah 29:11*

It is summertime and school is out. The weather is hot and sticky as normal, and Mom and Dad are sitting in the den watching television and trying to decide what they are going to do for summer vacation. Mom is a teacher and is out for summer vacation as well, so she decided to help with vacation bible school.

Dad says, "Well, you know, we have two weeks of vacation bible school, and then we can plan something after that."

Mom says, "Sounds good, love. Do you have anything in mind?"

Dad grins and looks at her and says, "Yup, you know I love the beach. Let's go somewhere where the water is blue, and we can just relax."

Mom says, "Sounds good to me. Well, I'm going into the work room so I can prepare my lessons for vacation bible school."

Dad says, "Okay, you must have forgotten that I will be teaching a fun class about how to make quick snacks when your parents are running late from work!"

Mom says, "That's right! I'm so excited for you."

Dad says, "Yes, I see the theme is vision."

Mom says, "Yes, the focal verse is *Jeremiah 29: 11*, My foundation scripture for my life."

Dad nods and says, "Yes, I agree."

As Mom walks down the hall, she peeks in Elise's room to see why she is so quiet.

Mom says, "I should have known!"

Elise laughs and says, "Yes, I see my class for vacation bible school, I'm so excited! I have my favorite teacher, and she makes learning about God so fun!"

Mama smiles and says, "Good, baby." She then proceeds to walk out.

Elise stops her and says, "Mama, help me read the focus scripture please."

Mama says, "Sure, it says, *'For I know the plans I have for you,' declares the LORD, 'plans to prosper you and not to harm you, plans to give you hope and a future' (Jeremiah 29:11)*".

Elise says, "Wow! Ma'am, what does this mean?"

Mama says, "It means that God loves us so much that he already knows our future. He has everything planned out for us, and that is not to harm us, but for us to do good."

Elise looks at her mom in amazement and says, "God is really powerful, and real."

Mama says, "Yes, He is real."

Elise did not have any more questions and begins to flip through the paperwork for vacation bible school. Mom walks back out and continues to her work room.

Elise beings to think, and she wonders what plans God has for her. She knows they will be good because that's what Mama says the scripture says. She can't wait because she knows Jesus loves her.

Prayer: Dear God, thank you in advance for the plans you have for my life. Amen.

Chapter 7

Who am I?
God of Completion

"Be confident of this, that he who began a good work in you will carry it on to completion until the day of Christ Jesus." Philippians 1:6

It is Friday evening, which means it is family night. Mom, Elise, and Dad are in the den preparing to watch a movie. Mom asks Dad what they are watching tonight.

He says, *"The Princess and theFrog."*

Elise yells, Thank you, Daddy," and hugs his neck.

He says, "Of course, baby girl."

Meanwhile, Mom walks back into the kitchen to finish popping the popcorn and preparing the other snacks. Dad comes back in and sits on a chair in the kitchen near the center of the kitchen.

He says, "Have you thought about what you are going to discuss at the conference?"

Mom says, "Yes, but I'm trying to put everything together."

Dad says, "What's your focal scripture?"

She says, *"Philippians 1:6. "*

Dad says, "Good one."

Mom says, "Yes, I will use my testimony about how God had to remove me from everyone and everything I love to remind me of His promises."

Dad says, "Yes, that is correct, honey, and He will do that. What else?"

Mom says, "That I have to remember, just because I cannot see it with my natural eye, nor do I understand, it does not mean that it won't happen."

"Exactly," he says.

"So, I used that scripture to remind us to be confident in what God has told you to do. Whether that it is to write a book, be an Entrepreneur, or preach the gospel. Whatever it is, just know that He is a God of completion, and He will finish what He started."

Dad says, "Great, I cannot wait to see how God continues to move in your life. He never ceases to amaze me."

Mom looks at him with a comforting grin, and says, "You're right, so get ready."

Dad laughs and walks back into the den, where Elise is with the snacks. Mom follows behind him with the drinks. They sit down and the movie starts. Elise in the middle, Mom is on one side and Dad on her other side.

Dad leans over and whispers in Mom's ear, "You got this."

Mom's heart flutters.

She says, "Thanks, baby, we got this. God, me, and you."

Elise looks up at the two of them with her finger over her lips to tell them she cannot hear. Mom and Dad laugh and proceed to watch the movie.

Dad whispers in Mom's ear, "God is a God of completion."

Mom nods slowly and says, "Don't I know."

Prayer: Dear God, thank you for doing a good work in me and completing it. Amen

Chapter 8

Who am I?
God of Faith

*"and without faith it is impossible to please
God, because anyone who comes to him must
believe that He exists and that he rewards
those who seek him." Hebrews 11: 6*

It is the first Sunday of the New Year, and Service is packed as usual. Today seems to be even more packed because the New Year always brings everyone back to church. Elise, Mom, and Dad pull up at church, and park their car. Dad goes ahead of Mom and Elise because he is the son of the house at the church, and he has to go to the pastor study.

Mom and Elise follow behind him but have to turn around and go back to the car because Elise left her bible. Elise attends church school, while Mom and Dad go into the big sanctuary.

Mom tells Elise, "Didn't I tell you to make sure you have everything before you got out of the car?"

Elise, says, "Yes, ma'am, I'm sorry."

The two continue into the church. Mom nods and greets a few people on the way into the building. Mom then sees her friend as she approaches Mom and Elise.

"Well, good morning ladies!" She then walks in front of Elise. Stooping down in front of her, she says, "Good morning beautiful!"

Elise says, "Good morning, Ms. Jane."

She says, "Well, don't you ladies look dolled up today!"

Mom smiles and says, "Well, thank you, Ms. Jane!" and proceeds down the hall to sign Elise in to children's church.

Mom and Elise arrive at the table. Mom greets Ms. Tucker, who says good morning, and proceeds to ask Mom if she can be a flag bearer for fifth Sunday praise report.

Mom says, "Of course, you know we will do whatever you need us to do."

Ms. Tucker says, "Elise, thank you."

Elise gives her a huge smile, takes her name tag, and puts it around her neck.

Ms. Tucker says, "Do you know the way to your class?"

Elise says, "Yes, ma'am."

Mom says, "See you after service, baby."

Elise skips down the hall to her class, her teacher greets her, and Elise takes a seat next to her friend.

"The lesson will begin shortly, today we will talk about Faith."

Classes and service have ended, and Dad shows up to pick Elise up from church school. Elise's eyes always light up when she sees her daddy. She runs down the hall and jumps into his arms.

Dad is standing with a big smile on his face. "Well, hello, daddy's baby."

She says, "Hey, Daddy," smiling and grabbing his hand as he put her back down to walk. "Where's Mom?"

He says, "Mom is talking, so we will wait on her and then walk to the car together. She will meet us at the end of the hall."

As soon as he signs Elise out, Mom is walking down the hall.

She says, "Ready!"

Mom, Elise, and Dad walk out of the church to the car.

On their ride home, Mom and Dad are talking about service, and they ask Elise what she learned.

She says, "Well, we learned about faith!"

Elise's parents' faces light up because that is what their sermon was about as well.

Elise says, "But you know I have some more questions. Mom and Dad look at each other and giggle.

"Of course!" They say at the same time.

Mom says, "Baby, what do you want to know?"

Elise says, "Well, Mom, I understand faith, but I . . . I don't understand faith."

Dad says, "Let us help you. Do you know how you sit down in a chair?"

Elise says impatiently, "Yes, ugh, yes! But what does that have to do with faith?"

Dad says, "Wait, let me explain. You know you sit down knowing that the chair is going to hold you, right?"

Elise says, "Yes."

"Well, faith is just like that. We cannot see it, but it is something we believe. We may not understand it, but if we just believe a little, like a small seed, God will do the rest."

Elise says, "Well, Daddy, I get that, but how do I know that I have faith? Where does it come from?"

Mom says, "Let me try. Elise, remember the first scripture I taught you about God loving the world? Well, your faith begins when you believe that God died on the cross for our sins."

Elise nods and says, "Okay, Mama, but I believe that, and I know that, but I still can't see faith."

Mom says, "You are correct. Faith is not something that we see, but we have it because of God, and who is He is. Think about this," Mom sits up straight and continues, "You know when we get on the plane and fly to Virginia to see your Uncle Nic?"

She says, "Yes."

"Well, we trust that the plane is going to get us there safely, right?"

Elise nods as she tries to follow what her mom is telling her.

Mom continues, "Well baby, that *is* faith. We trust and believe that we will arrive safely, and that is what God wants us to believe about Him. We have to trust that what we read in the bible, and what we learn at church about faith is true."

Elise says, "Wow, Mom, that's still a little confusing. But you know I will have more questions later."

Dad chimes in and says, "Yes, we know, and as you get older you will learn and understand His word more."

Elise nods, listening to her Dad.

He says, "Sometimes, we, as adults, still have more questions about faith, but we do not stop believing."

2 But I will send a fire upon Moab,
And it shall devour the [palaces] of Kerioth;
Moab shall die with [tumult],
With shouting and [trumpet] sound.

3 And I will cut off the judge [from] its midst,
And slay all its princes with him,"
Says the Lord.

4 Thus says the Lord:

"For three transgressions of Judah, and for four,
I will not turn away its punishment,
Because they have despised the law of the Lord,
And have not kept His commandments.
Their lies lead them astray,
Lies which their fathers followed.

5 But I will send a fire upon Judah,
And it shall devour the palaces of Jerusalem."

6 Thus says the Lord:

"For three transgressions of Israel, and for four,
I will not turn away its punishment,
Because they sell the righteous for silver,
And the poor for a pair of sandals.
7 They pant after the dust of the earth which is on the head of the poor,
And pervert the way of the humble.
A man and his father go in to the same girl,
To defile My holy name.
8 They lie down by every altar on clothes taken in pledge,
And drink the wine of the condemned in the house of their god.

9 Yet it was I who destroyed the Amorite before them,
Whose height was like the height of the cedars,
And he was as strong as the oaks;
Yet I destroyed his fruit above
And his roots beneath.
10 Also it was I who brought you up from the land of Egypt,
And led you forty years through the wilderness,
To possess the land of the Amorite.
11 I raised up some of your sons as prophets,
And some of your young men as Nazirites.
Is it not so, O you children of Israel?"
Says the Lord.

12 "But you gave the Nazirites wine to drink,
And commanded the prophets saying,
'Do not prophesy!'

13 "Behold, I am weighed down by you,
As a cart full of sheaves is weighed down.
14 Therefore flight shall perish from the swift,
The strong shall not strengthen his power,
Nor shall the mighty deliver himself;
15 He shall not stand who handles the bow,
The swift of foot shall not escape,
Nor shall he who rides a horse deliver himself.
16 The most courageous men of might
Shall flee naked in that day,"
Says the Lord.

3 Hear this word that the Lord has spoken against you, O children of Israel, against the whole family which I brought up from the land of Egypt, saying:

2 "You only have I known of all the families of the earth;
Therefore I will punish you for all your iniquities."

3 Can two walk together, unless they are agreed?

4 Will a lion roar in the forest, when he has no prey?
Will a young lion cry out of

3:12 a The Hebrew is uncertain.

Mom nods in agreement, and Elise sits back and looks out the window as they are turning into their neighborhood. They are almost home. Dad turns the music up and they ride quietly.

Prayer: Dear God, thank you for giving me faith even when I don't seem to understand. Amen

Chapter 9
Who am I?

God of Prayer
"Always keep praying" Thessalonians 5:17

It is a cool Wednesday autumn evening. Elise is at the hospital with her mom and dad. They just found out that Grandma was in an accident.

A car hit her head on and threw her out of the automobile. The family is sitting in the waiting room praying, and Mom's eyes are filled with water. Dad is holding her hand tightly; trying to comfort her and tells her it will be okay. Elise is sitting in the corner watching television. . . at least that is what her parents believe she is doing.

Really, she is praying to God.

She says to herself, "I know that this works, but I do not know how fast it works. Mama and Daddy pray all the time. I know they say to always pray."

Mom and Dad look out of the corners of their eyes, and they see Elise on her knees with her hands together. They walk over to join her.

They ask, "Can we join?"

Elise says, "Yes, I don't know what to say, but I know you both say I should pray."

They both nod slowly with their eyes full of tears.

Elise says, "Dear God, it is me, Elise. I'm not sure what to say, or how to say what I need to say, but all I know is that I am thankful, and my grandma needs you. My mama needs you, my daddy needs you, and Lord, most of all again, my grandma needs you. We don't know what happened, but please help her get better. I know that Papa says, 'You are a healer, Lord,' so heal my grandmother, Lord."

Elise sits quietly after her last statement, and then says, "Amen."

Mom and Dad both hug her, as they hug her, Dr. Nyarie comes out of surgery and says,

"Mr. and Mrs. Brown, your mother is fine. She will take some time to heal due to her age, but she will recover."

Elise peeks from behind her daddy's legs and says, "Thank you. I prayed."

Dr. Nayrie smiles and says, "Good, because kids pray too!"

Elise nods and says, "Yup."

A few seconds later, Mom's sister and brother walk into the lobby.

"What happened?"

Mom explains to them that their mother was in an accident.

Dr. Nayrie says, "She is in ICU and will be here for a few days so we can monitor her. She will need her rest."

The family nods together and says, "When can we see her?"

The doctor says, "You all can go in two at a time, but please allow her to rest." The family agrees, and they begin going in two at a time.

Mom, Elise, and Dad go in first and leave afterwards. Elise has school the next morning.

As they walked to the car, Elise says, "God answers prayers."

Mom and Dad smile.

Elise proceeds to say, "See, kids pray too!"

Prayer: Dear God, thank you for the gift of prayer. Amen

Chapter 10

Who am I?

God of Provision

"The lord is my shepherd I shall not want." Psalm 23 :1

It is a cool spring day. Elise comes home from
school, and her mom is sitting at the table with her
head in her hands. She sees a stack of papers in
front of her and proceeds to ask her Mom,

"Where is Dad and what's wrong?"

Mom tries to dry the tears from her eyes, and says,
"Nothing is the matter," as any mother would do to
keep her child from worrying.

Elise walks over to the backdoor, and sees her dad
doing yard work. She decided to go out of the side
door to chat with him. He waves as he pushes the
lawnmower up and down the backyard rows. Elise
knew something wasn't right, but she knew she
couldn't push it with her parents. So, she went back
inside and sat at the table to begin her homework.

Mom brought her a snack and begins cooking
dinner. Elise noticed that Mom only had one pot on
the stove. This was not normal when it came to
dinner time, but she did not say anything again. She
just smiled at Mom. Dad opens the side door and
enters, he is finished mowing the yard. He leaves
his shoes at the door, smiles at Mom, and asks Elise

how her day was at school. He talks to Elise for a bit, and then goes upstairs to shower.

Dad comes back down in the kitchen and goes to the stove to talk to mom.

They are whispering about something, and when they realized Elise was listening, they said,

"Baby girl, go wash your hands for dinner."

Elise says, "Okay," and goes to wash her hands.

They all sit down at the dinner table as a family as they normally did, so this was not strange, but there was this awkwardness Elise could not describe. She was thinking about every possible thing at this time because she wasn't a little girl anymore, she was a pre-teen, and she knew something just wasn't right. The family eats dinner and has small talk at the table. Dad asks everyone how their day was, and if they are ready for the three-day weekend.

It was Easter Sunday, so school and most places were out because Friday is a holiday as well.

Mom smiles and Dad looks at her, as to say, "What did I say wrong?"

Elise finished up her plate. She scraps the crumbs in the trash and goes to her room to get ready for bed. As she is was walking upstairs, she could hear Dad asking Mom, "Is everything okay?"

Mom says, "No, it is not."

She tells Dad that she is being laid off from her job, and this will put the family in a tight financial position.

Dad smiles, and says, "No worries, baby."

See, Dad is a retired veteran, so he does not work anyway, but he receives a disability check from the military. He just relaxes at home and works on his old cars in the garage.

Mom was working as a part-time instructor at the university nearby, as well as online. Elise decides not to go all the way up the stairs and sits in the middle so she could hear what they are saying.

Dad tells Mom, "Do not worry about it. It will not put us in a bind, you must have forgotten who we serve."

She says, "I know that, but look at these bills that are still not paid."

Dad says again, "I said, do not worry. 'The Lord is our shepherd I (we) shall not want.' Meaning, that he provides for us. I know you believe, and I know you know Him. So, what's the problem?"

They finish washing dishes together and, Elise can hear them walking to the sofa. Mom is talking and Dad listening attentively.

He says, "Okay, I understand all that, but you know that we are blessed. God always provides all our needs. We never miss a meal, we may run tight, but as long as we pay our tithes and continue to put Him first in our home. We do not have anything to worry about." He continues, "Are you sure they are going to lay you off?"

Mom looks at him and shrugs her shoulders like a little girl, "No, not really. I overheard two full-time instructors talking in the copy room."

Dad says, "So you have allowed Satan to plant that seed in your mind that you are getting fired, and you are going on pure speculation." Dad laughs, grabs Mom's hands, and says, "Let's pray. Dear, Heavenly Father, help my wife in her unbelief. Satan is trying to slip his way into my family and cause confusion, but I know that you are a God of order, and you told us that we are the head and not the tail. So, Father, I ask that you work it out for our good and give my wife peace in this. Help her where her faith seems to be wavering. In Jesus' name, Amen."

The both say amen in unison, and Dad hugs Mom and sits back on the sofa.

Mom begins to make her way back upstairs and then sees Elise sitting on the stairs.

She asks, "Were you sitting here the entire time?"

Elise begins to ask her mom about what Daddy means when he said ,not to worry when she is clearly worried.

Mom says, "Elise, you know that your dad is a faith walking man of God. He has to remind me sometimes, that God is a provider no matter what the situation looks like. There were times, before you were born, when we did not know what we were going to eat, or how we were going to pay different bills. But, one thing I can say is, that God is faithful, and has never, I mean *never*failed us yet."

Elise looks up at her mom and says, "I know," with tears in her eyes. She says, "I always feel this peace or comfort over me, Mama, and I can't explain it."

Mama smiles and looks at her baby girl nodding her head slowly.

"Don't I know." she says. She hugs her and tells her to go shower.

 Mom looks up towards heaven and says, "Lord, you have done it again. I don't know how, I don't know when, but I know you will work it out." Mom begins to recite the 23rd Psalm softly to herself as she walks to her bedroom to get ready for bed.

"The Lord is my shepherd I shall not want. He makes me to lie down in the green pastures; He leads me besides the still waters. He restores my soul; He leads me in the paths of righteousness for his name sake. Yeah, though I walk through the valley of the shadow of death, I will fear no evil; For You are with me; Your rod and Your staff, they comfort me. You prepare a table before me in the presence of my enemies; You anoint my head with oil; My cup runs over. Surely goodness and mercy shall follow me all the days of my life; and I will dwell in the house of the Lord Forever."

Prayer: Dear God, thank you for being a provider. Amen

ABOUT THE AUTHOR

Demeterius Meyers, is an Educator and a Woman after God's own heart. She has that crazy faith and knows that her readers have not seen anything YET!